Waiting

Dai
Advent an

Year C

Katherine L. Howard, O.S.B.

LITURGICAL PRESS

Collegeville, Minnesota

www.litpress.org

Nihil obstat: Robert C. Harren, *Censor deputatus.*

Imprimatur: ✠ John F. Kinney, Bishop of St. Cloud, Minnesota, April 6, 2006.

Cover design by Ann Blattner

ISSN 1550-803X

ISBN 13: 978-0-8146-2988-8
ISBN 10: 0-8146-2988-1

Introduction

We spend a good deal of our lives waiting—waiting for family members to get ready to go on a trip, waiting for the school bus, waiting in line at the grocery store, waiting for the weekend to come, waiting for the big game, waiting to see the doctor, waiting to find out what grade we got on the test, waiting for the baby to be born, waiting for wife, husband, dad or mother to get home from work, waiting for someone we love to return from a trip, waiting for our own vacation, waiting to see if we get an interview for that job we applied for. Often we get tired of waiting. Sometimes our waiting is filled with dread. Sometimes we joyfully anticipate the happy conclusion of our waiting.

Although some things don't turn out as planned or hoped for, our lives are also often punctuated with exuberant celebrations of the good things that do come. We get the job. Our birthday celebration with family and friends is a wonderful occasion. The vacation time we saved and planned for arrives with everybody involved geared-up and ready to go. A healthy baby arrives safely after nine long months.

There is, however, always something more we want, something else we long for and are willing to work for. That is the nature of human life.

The celebration of waiting, of coming, and of desiring more is what the Advent and Christmas season is about.

Whether conscious of it or not, all of us at some level are waiting for God, even while we celebrate the coming of God in the historical Jesus and in Christ's daily coming into our lives. Every kind of waiting is an opportunity for us to get in touch with this fundamental spiritual waiting. Every celebration of a joy fulfilled, a gift of life received, mirrors in some way that ultimate gift of God's Self coming to us in Christ. Every unfulfilled, increased or new desire is an echo of our deepest longing for ultimate fulfillment in the God whose daily coming is always more than we can take in, and whose coming will only be fully experienced at the end of our lives and our world.

During this Advent and Christmas season we are drawn into this spiritual dimension of that continual human cycle of waiting and longing, fulfillment, and the return and deepening of our waiting and desire. This is not a matter of going around in circles, but of moving in a kind of spiral always more deeply into Christ's life. His Spirit fills us with the longing that makes it possible for us to wait more patiently and with more hope for new manifestations of his presence in our lives. And our Spirit-filled longing helps us live joyfully trusting that in Christ we will be united in God forever when our time on earth comes to an end.

The Scripture readings for the season of Advent put us in touch with the sentiments and insights of the Old Testament prophets, of John the Baptist and Jesus' mother, Mary, as they looked forward to the historical coming of God incarnate in Jesus. As we recall their joyful hope we look forward with anticipation to our Christmas celebration of its fulfillment, and we let their experience stir up our hope for Christ's coming within and around us daily and in his final glorious coming. The Christmas and Epiphany readings make present the mystery and joy surrounding Jesus birth, and the revelation of God's Self to the world through him. They celebrate God's becoming human like us and staying with us. The gospel readings especially, both those of Advent and Christmas, open us to the words and actions of Jesus himself as he comes into our lives and invites us to hope in him.

At every Eucharist after the Our Father, the presider leads us in prayer that we may be protected "from all anxiety as we wait in joyful hope for the coming of our Savior, Jesus Christ." As we read Scripture and celebrate Eucharist this season of Advent and Christmas, may our faith that God has come in the historical Jesus and remains with us in the Spirit of the Risen Christ fill us with that "joyful hope." May we be freed "from all anxiety" as we wait for Christ's coming in ourselves, others, and the events of each day, and as we look forward to his glorious coming at the end of our lives and the end of time. May our openness to Christ's coming help transform our world through his Love, which is the source of our joy now and will be forever.

Katherine L. Howard, O.S.B.

FIRST WEEK OF ADVENT

December 3: Sunday of the First Week of Advent

Strengthen Your Hearts

Readings: Jer 33:14-16; 1 Thess 3:12–4:2; Luke 21:25-28, 34-36

Scripture:
Jesus said to his disciples:
"Beware that your hearts do not become drowsy
    from carousing and drunkenness
    and the anxieties of daily life. . . .
Be vigilant at all times
    and pray that you have the strength
    . . . to stand before the Son of Man" (Luke 21:25, 34a, 36).

Reflection: Beginnings can be exciting, challenging, exhilarating: starting school, entering a new year, taking on a new job, welcoming a new baby. Putting out the final effort to bring something to completion can bring a rush of energy too: that last effort to finish a race, burning the midnight oil to put the period on a school or work project. Even keeping that final vigil with a dying loved one can call forth extraordinary energy we gladly expend and barely notice. But middles, including the middle of life, tend to feel long, to drag on. Weariness, boredom, confusion, anxiety can weigh us down. We are tempted to give up, turn back, quit. We feel that we could easily succumb to anything that will help us escape. "Carousing and drunkenness" (Luke 21:34) can seem like a pretty good option! Today's gospel addresses these midlife doldrums.

Jesus is concerned that our hearts may become so "drowsy from carousing and drunkenness and the anxieties of daily life" (Luke 21:34) that we will not "have the strength . . . to stand before the Son of Man" on that final day of his coming. Though we may not be around to experience 'that day' at the end of the world, we certainly will know it at the moment of our death. If we are to stand before Christ then with strength of heart, we need some daily strengthening now.

What are the daily exercises that will get us in shape? In the second reading St. Paul gives us more than a clue. He prays: "May the Lord make you increase and abound in love for one another and for all . . . so as to strengthen your hearts . . . at the coming of our Lord Jesus . . ." (1 Thess 3:12-13). Daily, and many times daily, during all the in-between years of life we can call on the Spirit of Christ living within us to pour out divine love through our unique personalities and communities, increasing our love for one another and all people. If in all circumstances we are praying, "Come, Lord Jesus" (Rev 22:20b), that will be the joyful prayer in our hearts, if not on our lips, as we greet him on 'that day.'

Meditation: Welcome God's presence and action into your life and activity as many times today as you remember to do so. Pray simply and without anxiety: "Come, Lord Jesus," or some short phrase that comes to mind.

Prayer: Saving God, you strengthen our hearts by showing us your love at work in our lives and in our world in the daily comings of Jesus Christ. In this strength may we persevere until his final coming in death. This we pray in his name. Amen.

December 4: Monday of the First Week of Advent

The Kingdom of Heaven

Readings: Isa 2:1-5; Matt 8:5-11

Scripture:
[Jesus] . . . said to those following him,
"Amen, I say to you, in no one in Israel have I found
such faith.
I say to you, many will come from the east and the west,
and will recline with Abraham, Isaac, and Jacob
at the banquet in the Kingdom of heaven. . . ." (Matt
8:10b-11).

Reflection: The kingdom of heaven—God's reign—is a dominant theme in the Gospel of Matthew. In today's passage Jesus speaks of that reign in terms of a great banquet to come in the future, a metaphor from Isaiah the prophet familiar to the Jewish people of Jesus' time. When the divine plans are fulfilled "the LORD of hosts will provide for all peoples a feast of rich food and choice wines" (Isa 25:6). And according to Jesus the people coming to that great banquet will be from "east and west," that is, from all the ends of the earth, not just those like us! Isaiah declares that the divine messianic banquet is for "all nations" (Isa 2:2b). Sometimes, in fact, it is the people who are unlike us—those from "east and west"—those we least expect, even the nonreligious people, like the centurion of today's gospel, who recognize the reign of God more readily than we do, and show us how to open up to it.

The centurion sets aside any claim to his own worthiness and professes his complete willingness to depend solely on the goodness and effectiveness of Jesus' word to put into effect the healing power of the divine reign. That, Jesus says, is real faith! Today's gospel invites us to watch for the centurions in our lives, perhaps those seemingly nonreligious neighbors who, like the centurion, in their concern for others in need, recognize the resources available to help them, and solicit their assistance. The gospel invites us to follow their example not only individually but as families, parishes, communities, and nations. In whatever people and agencies we find loving generosity and concern for suffering humanity, there is the healing presence of God whether explicitly acknowledged or not. The eyes of faith see God's reign where there is generous love. Responding in faith to that reign will bring us all together into its future fulfillment.

Meditation: What suffering individuals and peoples are on your mind? Setting aside any doubts about your own worthiness, ask Jesus in faith to speak his word of healing on their behalf.

Prayer: Generous God, giver of all good gifts and healing balm of all who are afflicted, touch all who are suffering, particularly those for whom we now pray, through the healing Spirit of your Word, Jesus Christ. Amen.

December 5: Tuesday of the First Week of Advent

Joy in the Holy Spirit

Readings: Isa 11:1-10; Luke 10:21-24

Scripture:
Jesus rejoiced in the Holy Spirit and said,
   "I give you praise, Father, Lord of heaven and earth,
   for although you have hidden these things
   from the wise and the learned
   you have revealed them to the childlike" (Luke 10:21a).

Reflection: In the gospel passage just preceding today's, the
disciples return to Jesus rejoicing because of the power they
have exercised over demons in his name. Jesus tells them
that he was aware of what had been going on, and that, yes,
their power over demons did come from him (Luke 10:17-19).
But, he adds, don't focus so much on that, but rather on the
fact that "your names are written in heaven" (Luke 10:20).
In other words, don't be too easily overinflated about what
you accomplish, even with my help, but stay in tune with
the most central reality in your lives, your life in God. This
life in God is the source of Jesus' joy and of ours.

   It could be that God as Trinity seems to us more like an
intellectual puzzle than anything touching our lives. And
talk about "knowledge of God" may seem abstract and weari-
some. On the other hand, there is no joy in life as rich as that
of loving and being loved: giving one's whole self and life

to another by whom one is totally accepted, and welcoming and embracing the total return of the other in love. The knowledge Jesus is speaking about—that knowledge the Father has of the Son and the Son of the Father—is the divine experience of such total, mutual, self-giving love, that love which is the Holy Spirit. It is love that freely shares "all things" (Luke 10:22). Translated into Jesus' and our human experience, that means love so unconditional and generous it shares its every thought, feeling, sorrow, joy with us!

In his total receptivity to the Father's life and love poured out in him, Jesus is the source and living demonstration of what God's coming in him is meant to do for us: unite us with him and one another in childlike dependence and openness to the total, unconditional, never-failing love of God. In and with Jesus our lives are meant to radiate that gift of Love and resonate with spontaneous joy in the Holy Spirit. This is more important than anything we will ever accomplish.

Meditation: With childlike confidence ask Jesus through the power of the Holy Spirit to open you to know God's unconditional love. Return throughout the day to trust in that love.

Prayer: Come, Holy Spirit, open our hearts to the divine life and love in which Jesus rejoices. Draw us together more deeply into that life today and every day so that his joy may be ours. Amen.

December 6: Wednesday of the First Week of Advent

Our Tender-hearted God

Readings: Isa 25:6-10a; Matt 15:29-37

Scripture:
Jesus summoned his disciples and said,
   "My heart is moved with pity for the crowd,
   for they have been with me now for three days
   and have nothing to eat.
I do not want to send them away hungry
   for fear they may collapse on the way" (Matt 15:32).

Reflection: When people stop at our homes or apartments to visit and our welcome is sincere, the surroundings pleasant, the conversation engaging, we may lose track of time. When mealtime sneaks up on us, we do not want to send our guests away, especially if they have come to share some burden, find company in their loneliness or sorrow, or to get some support or advice in difficulty. Even though we may have missed our regular trip to the grocery that week, our minds work creatively to think of something we might serve that will satisfy their hunger. And we insist that they stay to share even the little we have.

The God Jesus has come to manifest is the quintessential generous, sensitive and loving host who would never send anyone in need away without having fed them, lest they grow weak on the way. He comes to reveal the God Isaiah speaks of in the first reading, the one who "will provide for all peoples a feast of rich food and choice wines, juicy, rich food and pure, choice wines" (Isa 25:6b).

God is like a sensitive, compassionate, generous, caring and resourceful mother. Jesus, embodying these motherly qualities, invites us today to come to him just as we are with our own hungers, and also to bring with us those in our families and communities, in our nation and world who are lame, blind, deformed, without voice—and hungry—all those in need of his help. His heart continues to be "moved with pity for the crowd" (Matt 15:32a). He will feed us, and he also invites us, as he invites the disciples in today's gospel, to share what we have, little though it may seem to us, with those who have needs as great, or greater, than ours.

Meditation: Think of some way in which you are hungry. Think also of some among your local and global neighbors who need to be fed. Entrust yourself and them to Jesus in prayer, and ask him sincerely what you can do to help.

Prayer: O God, generous host and mother of the human family, thank you for providing food for our hungry bodies and souls in Jesus. Fill us with the sensitivity and generosity of his Spirit so that your love may touch others through us. Amen.

Lord, Lord

Readings: Isa 26:1-6; Mt 7:21, 24-27

Scripture:
Jesus said to his disciples:
  "Not everyone who says to me, 'Lord, Lord,'
  will enter the Kingdom of heaven,
  but only the one who does the will of my Father in
    heaven" (Matt 7:21).

Reflection: Do you remember the last time you sat among a group of friends or acquaintances solving the neighbors' problems with their children, the country's problems with its energy policy and transportation system, the parish's problem with its faith formation program? Someone may have interjected or even ended the conversation with the phrase, "Talk is cheap!" On another occasion you may have addressed some particularly critical person suggesting that he or she, "Put your money where your mouth is!" We are all familiar with these common phrases, and we know what they mean. Words might sound good. They may even convey a certain measure of intellectual truth. But if words are not supported by the will to act, they are ineffective.

Conversation with another person can be empty too. We might say all the right words, but make no sincere, heartfelt connection with the inner core of the other at a deeper level of understanding and will. Our words then are lightweight—like feathers flying away in the wind rather than fruitful seeds from our heart that take root in the heart of the other and grow into a living connection between us.

The same is true of our communication with God in Christ. Prayer is a matter of more than the mouth, even more than the intellect. It is a matter of the heart—and that taken in the biblical sense of 'heart' as the central core of our person including thinking, feeling, willing. To be effective in uniting us with the kingdom of heaven, that is, the divine coming in our lives here and now, as well as in the future, our prayer must come out of the central core of our being. The proof of such heartfelt prayer is our willingness to live in accord with the sentiments we express in prayer. Empty words, unsupported by loving action, mean nothing. Light as feathers they float away on the breeze. Only the weight and energy of effective love carries them straight as an arrow to their destination in God's heart.

Meditation: Reflect on your prayer and actions during the last twenty-four hours. Are they in harmony? Do they come out of a desire to live according to God's will? With faith and trust, open to God's loving will in your life now and ask that all your actions today be in harmony with God's will.

Prayer: Jesus, you are the desire of all nations. Help us live in harmony with your loving will so that we call upon you always in sincerity of heart. Amen.

December 8: Solemnity of the Immaculate Conception
(Catholic Church)

Friday of the First Week of Advent
(Episcopal Church)

Handmaids

Readings: Gen 3:9-15, 20; Eph 1:3-6, 11-12; Luke 1:26-38

Scripture:
Mary said, "Behold, I am the handmaid of the Lord.
May it be done to me according to your word."
Then the angel departed from her (Luke 1:38).

Reflection: Mary was free from original sin. That is the doctrinal meaning of the Feast of the Immaculate Conception. Theologians and everyday Christians have for many centuries struggled to understand the meaning of original sin. As children we were probably all satisfied with quite a literal interpretation of the Genesis story—that Adam and Eve, the first man and woman, disobeyed God by actually eating the 'forbidden fruit.' From then on all their descendants, including all of us, were bound to sin, to suffer and to die. Most of us have developed some theological understanding of that story since then, but still wonder what it really means.

What makes the most sense to me now is thinking of original sin as our experience of coming to full human self-consciousness without the realization that we are united with

God in love. God who is Love cannot withhold God's self from us. Our deepest reality is good and united with God and others in love. Because we come to full human self-consciousness without realizing that, we are deeply insecure. We set out to find our security in distorted ways: through excessive drives for possessions, for affection and esteem, for power and control. We do not want to be God's handmaids. Nor can we be until we realize in faith that God's unconditional love blesses "us in Christ with every spiritual blessing in the heavens" (Eph 1:3b).

In some implicit way from the very beginning of her life, Mary had this certitude in faith. Because of that she was able to be "the handmaid of the Lord" (Luke 1:38), the joyous, willing recipient of God's love, and a full participant in God's creative and redeeming work.

Through faith and Baptism we have come with Mary to the certitude that we also are united to God in the love of Christ. We too, then, are able to say joyfully with her today, "Behold I am the handmaid of the Lord. May it be done to me according to your word" (Luke 1:38).

Meditation: With Mary rejoice and rest in God's unconditional love. If you doubt this reality, ask God to strengthen your faith.

Prayer: Gracious God, in your goodness and love give us faith like Mary's. Rejoicing in your goodness and ours, may we awaken others to your love. We pray in Christ Jesus. Amen.

December 9: Saturday of the First Week of Advent

Leadership in God's Reign

Readings: Isa 30:19-21, 23-26; Matt 9:35–10:1, 5a, 6-8

Scripture:
At the sight of the crowds, [Jesus'] heart was moved with
   pity for them,
   because they were troubled and abandoned,
   like sheep without a shepherd.
Then he summoned his Twelve disciples
   and gave them authority over unclean spirits to drive
      them out
   and to cure every disease and every illness (Matt 9:36;
      10:1).

Reflection: God's compassion and power to heal are manifested in today's gospel in the action of Jesus. Jesus responded to the troubled and abandoned crowds with sensitive feeling. But his response did not stop there. It included intelligent and reflective thought and effective action. Had Jesus not been sensitive he would not have cared that people were aimless and suffering. Had he not been intelligent and reflective, he would have had no idea what to do. Had he not been willing to take action, whether intelligent, reflective and sensitive, he would not have had the energy and drive to do anything about it. Jesus has the qualities of a good leader: empathy, insightful awareness that comes out of intelligent reflection, and the energy and organizational skills for effective action. In addition he has another necessary quality of good leadership: he empowers others to share that leadership by taking on his mission as their own.

Among the troubled and abandoned Jesus sees in the crowds today are those who have lost homes and loved ones in wars, hurricanes, floods, earthquakes, mudslides, etc. Thousands of children are enslaved as prostitutes or laborers; millions of people are addicted to drugs and alcohol; countless numbers of adults are without meaningful work or a living wage. These are our neighbors, our family members, our friends, ourselves. Jesus lives in our world moved with pity for all who are "troubled and abandoned." He heals us and enlists our help to heal others. He empowers us with his own divine compassion and sensitivity, his insight, and his courage to take action, his Spirit.

Meditation: Reflect on ways you have been healed and empowered by the leadership of others and the ways your leadership has helped heal and empower others. Give thanks to God for Christ's work through them and you.

Prayer: Compassionate God, you have come to live among us as healer and life-giver in your Son Jesus. Open our eyes and ears to his compassionate, intelligent, effective, and empowering presence in ourselves and in all who share our planet. This we pray in his name. Amen.

SECOND WEEK OF ADVENT

Deserts

Readings: Bar 5:1-9; Phil 1:4-6, 8-11; Luke 3:3-6

Scripture:
In the fifteenth year of the reign of Tiberius Caesar,
    when Pontius Pilate was governor of Judea,
    and Herod was tetrarch of Galilee, . . .
    during the high priesthood of Annas and Caiaphas,
    the word of God came to John the son of Zechariah in
        the desert (Luke 3:1-2).

Reflection: The times and places that open us to hearing the word of God are not always comfortable or comforting. "[T]he word of God came to John the son of Zechariah in the desert" while "Pontius Pilate was governor of Judea, and Herod was tetrarch of Galilee," and "during the high priesthood of Annas and Caiaphas" (Luke 3:1-2). That desert was a hot, dry, harsh place which tested body and spirit. And the Herod spoken of here would soon have John beheaded. He, Pontius Pilate, and the high priests would be key players in the suffering and death of Jesus. Because John had lots of reflection time during his desert days, he was probably aware of these possibilities— whether in a kind of subliminal way or more consciously.

Adversity can play a key role in honing our ability to hear what is beyond the usual scope of our ordinary consciousness. Facing a terminal illness, for example, may bring a person to a deep appreciation of the wonderful gifts each moment of life brings. As eighteenth century writer Samuel Johnson put it, "Depend upon it, sir, when a man knows he is to be hanged in a fortnight, it concentrates his mind wonderfully." It is precisely for such clarity and insight that people seek out desert experiences such as solitary retreats in which they step away from many of the usual supports of life—family, friends, familiar surroundings, and regular routine—in order to be open to God's call.

Whether we choose desert times and places or whether they are provided for us by life in the form of sickness, shifting employment or loss of job, failures in relationships, deaths of loved ones, difficulties in prayer, doubts about faith, these deserts hold new possibilities for our hearing the word of God at ever deepening levels. When the environment around us shifts and becomes unfamiliar, even harsh, we have the opportunity to let our spiritual ears perk up in order to tune in to God's voice on wavelengths that previously escaped our awareness.

Meditation: Take some time today to let yourself become aware of any way that you are in the desert. Open to the feelings this brings up in you, welcome them and in faith, if with God's grace you are able, welcome God's presence in this experience.

Prayer: Faithful God, you have come to be with us in all our experiences of life. Through the Spirit of Christ risen and coming into our lives at every moment deepen our trust in your love, especially in the adversities of our lives. This we pray for ourselves and all people. Amen.

December 11: Monday of the Second Week of Advent

Paralysis

Readings: Isa 35:1-10; Luke 5:17-26

Scripture:
"But that you may know
    that the Son of Man has authority on earth to forgive sins"—
he said to the one who was paralyzed,
    "I say to you, rise, pick up your stretcher, and go home"
    (Luke 5:24).

Reflection: I have never been physically paralyzed and hope never to be. Sometimes, though, I have experienced a kind of inner paralysis that makes it all but impossible to think, to feel, to connect with others. Such an experience, as you yourself may well know, can be terrifying. One has responsibilities, commitments, duties, deadlines to meet that seem absolutely impossible to fulfill. In such a condition no willpower is available to lift even one little finger of effort in that direction. It is a helpless state that is debilitating like physical paralysis. When one is paralyzed—either physically or interiorly—it does no good to deny it. Some power has to come from beyond the limits of our paralyzed self to help us, at least to move, and optimally to free us from the paralysis itself.

Fear is the source of our emotional, intellectual, and spiritual paralysis—a fear so great we may better call it terror or dread. It rises out of a deep insecurity, which is our psychological experience of original sin. All of us come into full human self-consciousness without realizing that we are embraced in the unconditional love of God and are connected in that love with one another. Feeling alone and afraid we cope in ways that are destructive for ourselves and others. Most of the time we keep ourselves so busy that we are unaware of this. Sometimes the deep fear breaks through in ways that get our attention! Like St. Paul we feel the paralysis: "For I do not do the good I want, but I do the evil I do not want. Now if [I] do what I do not want, it is no longer I who do it, but sin that dwells in me" (Rom 7:19-20).

The only real cure for this inner paralysis is the deep experiential knowledge of God's healing power with and in us in Christ who is saying: "As for you, your sins are forgiven" (Luke 5:20), and "I say to you, rise, pick up your stretcher, and go home" (Luke 5:26). God's healing power is coming to us today through and in this gospel passage, in life. We celebrate that in today's Eucharist. To open to it we have only to accept our condition and say sincerely "I/We need your help."

Meditation: Today let yourself become aware of whatever might be paralyzing you. Let yourself feel it. Accept it. Breathe deeply. In a simple act of faith reaffirm your trust in the unconditional loving presence of Jesus, God-with-us. Welcome his presence and healing love.

Prayer: Jesus, healer of our paralysis, let us know your presence in our lives so that free from fear we may love you above and in all things and freely give your love to others. We pray this in your name. Amen.

December 12: Feast of Our Lady of Guadalupe
(Catholic Church)

Tuesday of the Second Week of Advent
(Episcopal Church)

Hill Country

Readings: Zech 2:14-17 or Rev 11:19a; 12:1-6ab; Luke 1:26-38 or Luke 1:39-47

Scripture:
Mary set out
    and traveled to the hill country in haste
    to a town of Judah,
    where she entered the house of Zechariah
    and greeted Elizabeth (Luke 1:39-40).

Reflection: Mary evidently had no aversion to climbing hills, to navigating the back country, nor to tackling less traveled roads and paths. She set out shortly after the beginning of her own pregnancy to visit her cousin Elizabeth in the hill country of Judah. The hills there rise up to 3,000 feet above sea level and its valleys are deep. Whether on the back of a donkey or walking she would have had to be in pretty good shape to say nothing of the courage it would take to face the perils of the road—dust and wind, heat and cold, steep climbs and, perhaps, robbers. She, of course, was highly motivated— overjoyed to share the good news of God's loving compassion with Elizabeth and to hear about her cousin's unexpected good fortune of becoming pregnant in her old age. That would have kept her going when things got tough.

In December of 1531, Mary traveled to hill country again, in Mexico. (The trip—this time from her heavenly home—I dare say, was a bit easier!) According to the sixteenth century account of the apparitions of Our Lady of Guadalupe, Juan Diego, a poor Indian, first became aware of Mary's presence when at Tepeyac hill he heard singing like that of beautiful birds. A voice at the top of the hill called him and he climbed up. There she was, an Aztec Lady more lovely than any human woman with garments shining like the sun. She asked that a church be built there so that in that hill country she could continue to pour out God's compassion and love, to give help and protection.

Mary continues to devote her life to sharing the compassion and love of God, which extends to everyone. No hill is too steep for that love to climb. No person is too poor to receive it. In fact, Mary and her son seem to feel particularly at home in the back country, in the hills, with the poor.

Meditation: Everyone is poor in some way. In what way do you feel poor? Ask God to help you find what you need so that you may give generously to others.

Prayer: Compassionate God, you hear the cries of the poor. Help us and all our suffering sisters and brothers in our material and spiritual poverty. Through your son Jesus strengthen us so that we may be compassionate to others. We pray in Jesus' name. Amen.

Come and Rest

Readings: Isa 40:25-31; Matt 11:28-30

Scripture:
Jesus said to the crowds:
"Come to me, all you who labor and are burdened,
  And I will give you rest" (Matt 11:28).

Reflection: Trying hard is a lesson most of us learned early in life. According to the old adage, "If at first you do not succeed, try again." Of course, it is important to try, to make efforts to accomplish goals, to carry out our duty, to improve our character, etc. . . . Without expending some effort, without engaging in productive labor, we not only fail to contribute what we can to our world and our time, but our brains and bodies would deteriorate from lack of activity.

In the spiritual life trying is also important. We need to do our part to let go sinful habits, those attitudes and actions that are destructive for ourselves, others, and our world. We also need to do good by cultivating a life of Christian service and prayer. However, after some success (with God's grace) in our efforts on this spiritual path, we usually come to places where our labors fail. Trying harder to love a neighbor we experience as aggravating, working to rid ourselves of prejudice, putting more effort into ways of praying that used to work but now seem to get us nowhere—such expenditure of energy begins to be not only useless, but counterproductive. We get discouraged and want to quit. We are weary and burdened.

At times like these I like to remember how Johnny Carson on his show many years ago reported the response of a child to a teacher's request to complete the saying, "If at first you don't succeed. . . ." The child's immediate and unhesitating reply was, "They'll help you." This is the attitude Jesus is inviting us to take in today's gospel. You don't have to do it all by yourself, he says. In fact, I will do it for and in you, if you let me. There are times when resting, not trying harder, is the solution. Jesus invites us to stop and rest, to loosen our desperate grip on our need to succeed by our own power, and to let his Spirit fill us with peace and whatever energy we need to do his will.

Meditation: In what ways are you weary and burdened, and trying too hard? Take a little time to give any frustration or discouragement about this over to God who is with you coming into your life in Jesus through his Spirit. Rest in God.

Prayer: Jesus, you alone can free us from our excessive and unnecessary labors. Receive us now as we come to you for that deep interior rest that will make our burdens light as we carry them with you. We pray through the inspiration of your Spirit. Amen.

December 14: Thursday of the Second Week of Advent

Violence and the Kingdom

Readings: Isa 41:13-20; Matt 11:11-15

Scripture:
"From the days of John the Baptist until now,
the Kingdom of heaven suffers violence,
and the violent are taking it by force" (Matt 11:12).

Reflection: From the time he began his public ministry—after the imprisonment of John the Baptist—Jesus preached "Repent, for the kingdom of heaven is at hand" (Matt 4:17b). "Kingdom of heaven" is Matthew's term for the reign of God, that golden age of peace and love when "the wolf shall be the guest of the lamb" and "the calf and the young lion shall browse together" (Isa 11:6). Jesus, the Messiah, is the Prince of Peace (Isa 9:5), who embodied that reign in himself and spent his earthly life proclaiming it in word and deed.

However, the announcement of this reign met with violent resistance. Jesus' identification of himself with the poor, the weak, the sinner—and his work for the justice, healing, and forgiveness necessary to spread this reign of peace brought him resistance, insult, arrest, torture, and a cruel death. In his very person "the Kingdom of heaven suffer[ed] violence and the violent [took it] by force." Jesus, however, did not respond with violence. His peaceful response of unconditional love, persevering through terrible suffering, burst through that violence in his resurrection and the pouring out of his Spirit of peace and love within all creation.

The "now" that Jesus is talking about in today's gospel was the "now" of his historical lifetime, but it is also the "now" of today. Our unjust, violent attitudes and actions toward ourselves produce violent attitudes and actions toward others. Our personal injustice and our unjust social and economic systems do violence to the poor, the sick, the oppressed. This breeds violent responses in them. The "Kingdom of heaven" continues to suffer violence; we are still driving it away by force. But the peaceful reign of God's love is also still coming into our lives in the Prince of Peace. It breaks through in our repentance, our turning around and accepting that reign when we stop the violence and work for justice, healing, and reconciliation in our personal and societal lives. In us Jesus continues to respond with non-violent resistance to evil. The transforming power of the Prince of Peace lives within us in his Spirit of love.

Meditation: Let yourself become aware of your violent attitudes toward yourself and toward other individuals or groups. As you are able with God's grace, give them over to the transforming Spirit of Christ within you, the Prince of Peace.

Prayer: Prince of Peace, you have come and are coming into our world to bring us into harmony in your reign of peace. Open our hearts in welcome to your loving presence which alone can free us from hatred, injustice and violence. We pray in your name. Amen.

Wisdom

Readings: Isa 48:17-19; Matt 11:16-19

Scripture:
" . . . John came neither eating nor drinking, and they
    said,
  'He is possessed by a demon.'
The Son of man came eating and drinking and they said,
  'Look, he is a glutton and a drunkard,
  a friend of tax collectors and sinners.'
But wisdom is vindicated by her works" (Matt 11:18-19).

Reflection: Jesus' lifestyle was quite unlike that of John, the strict ascetic who ate and drank sparingly. During his public ministry Jesus often joined others for meals and banquets like the one he shared at the tax collector's house after he had invited Matthew to follow him (Matt 9:9-13). Neither way of life seemed acceptable to the people: John, they said, was "possessed by a demon" and Jesus was "a glutton," "a drunkard" (Matt 11:18b, 19b). In the face of this criticism the gospel writer asserts that "wisdom is vindicated by her works" (Matt 11:19).

Among the works of wisdom is that of providing a feast and inviting the poor and the simple to come and dine. Wisdom, often personified in the Old Testament as the feminine aspect of the divine, "[builds] herself a house" and "[spreads] her table."

[S]he calls from the heights out over the city:
. . . "Come, eat of my food,
and drink of the wine I have mixed!" (Prov 9:1-3, 5).

In today's passage Jesus identifies himself, the Son of Man, as Wisdom, affirming that his actions will be vindicated by Wisdom's work in and through him.

Jesus as Wisdom provides the messianic banquet. He dines not only with those perceived as upright, but especially with tax collectors and sinners. This banquet is meant for all of us. In the messianic reign begun in Christ, he gives himself as food and drink for us in Eucharist. Strengthened by this food we journey on in hope and expectation of that final joyful messianic banquet in the life to come.

Meditation: Recall with confidence that Christ, Wisdom incarnate, lives in you, inviting you to eat and drink at the banquet. Give thanks for the material, intellectual, emotional, and spiritual food you are receiving and for all who daily share that food with you.

Prayer: Wisdom incarnate, we rejoice in the generosity of your banquet. Fill our hearts with that same generosity toward all in the various ways we share the meal of our lives with others. We pray with trust in your loving presence. Amen.

Elijah and John

Readings: Sir: 48:1-4, 9-11; Matt 17:9a, 10-13

Scripture:
[Jesus] said in reply,
". . . I tell you that Elijah has already come,
and they did not recognize him but did to him whatever
they pleased.
So also will the Son of Man suffer at their hands" (Matt
17:11-12).

Reflection: Elijah the prophet's abrupt disappearance in a flaming chariot (2 Kgs 2:11) had given rise among the Israelites to expectation that he would return as a forerunner of the "day of the Lord," the day that would usher in the messianic age (Mal 3:1, 23). Jesus tells his disciples today "that Elijah has already come, and they did not recognize him but did to him whatever they pleased" (Matt 17:12)—a veiled but pointed reference to John the Baptist as the returning Elijah. Jesus had begun his own public ministry at the time of John's arrest (Matt 4:12), and had retreated temporarily into the wilderness when John was killed (Matt 14:13). He knew that if people did not recognize and accept the one who came to announce the Messiah's presence, they would not recognize and accept him either.

Every day myriads of messengers arrive announcing God's coming in Christ: the woman at the bus stop whose smile we did not notice; the crippled man in the supermarket checkout line whom we did not see; the lyric soprano on public radio whose song we were too distracted to appreciate. The challenging student, the needy child, the wrong number. Each one comes not just to announce the future arrival of Christ but as his embodied presence now.

What keeps us from noticing? Maybe we are too fussy to see the gift before us, too worried about our lives to notice, too weary to care. Would you recognize the forerunner of God if you saw her? Would you recognize Christ if he appeared? Or is she too strange, too skinny, too dirty, too extreme? Is he too ascetic, too indulgent, too fat? Too poorly dressed, too well dressed? Too stupid, too smart?

All of us have at times passed by not just the forerunner, but the Messiah in our midst. The good news is that the Messiah keeps coming, and today we can with God's help take notice!

Meditation: Whom did you pass by, cut off, or ignore today who might have announced Christ's presence to you?

Prayer: Searcher of hearts, you are aware of our blind spots and prejudices. Please open the eyes of our minds and hearts so that we may not miss or pass by those whom you send into our lives as your messengers. We pray this with longing to recognize and welcome the coming of the Messiah today. We pray in his Spirit. Amen.

THIRD WEEK OF ADVENT

December 17: Sunday of the Third Week of Advent

Repent

Readings: Zeph 3:14-18a; Phil 4:4-7; Luke 3:10-18

Scripture:
The crowds asked John the Baptist,
  "What then should we do?" (Luke 3:10).

Reflection: What moved the crowds to ask John the Baptist this question? According to Luke's gospel, just prior to this John had been going about "the whole region of the Jordan proclaiming a baptism of repentance for the forgiveness of sins" (Luke 3:3). The crowds, either moved by his preaching or by their own curiosity, "came out to be baptized by him" (Luke 3:7). Before John would baptize though, he tested the sincerity of their desire for true repentance by naming their hypocrisy, calling them "a brood of vipers," and questioning their motives for fleeing "from the coming wrath" (Luke 3:7). Only "good fruits" will be "evidence of your repentance," he says (Luke 3:8).

"What then should we do?" they respond—a perfect opening for John to lay out the demands of the reign of God: share your material possessions with those who are more in need than you are, stop cheating, don't falsely accuse others or grumble when there is no justifiable grounds to do so. But do not for one minute think my baptism or your efforts will free you. The Messiah, who is mightier than I, is coming. It is he who will thoroughly purify you, burning away through the fire of the Spirit the chaff, dead roots and stubble of your sinful past. I, John, can proclaim his coming and tell you how to prepare, but it is he who will work the change in you.

Today we are the crowds captivated by the preaching of John the Baptist and we are asking "What should we do?" (Luke 3:10). We get the same answer. If you are really sincere about repentance, share your goods with those in need, don't cheat, don't lie, don't grumble. But know it is only the burning love of God's Spirit in Christ coming into your life that will free you from sin and fill you with the generous love to do this.

Graced by John's words in the gospel we begin. It is God's gift, the Spirit of Christ, who transforms us in the fire of divine love. That love pierces our hearts and changes our lives.

Meditation: In what way do John the Baptist's words invite you to change? Invite the loving Spirit of Christ within you for light to know what you must do and for the love and courage to do it, remembering that wisdom, love, and courage are gifts of that Spirit who lives within you.

Prayer: Spirit of Christ, you are a cleansing fire and a healing warmth within us. Cleanse and heal our wounded spirits stirring up in us your gifts of wisdom, love and courage so that we may live and act with integrity, justice and generosity. We pray this with trust in your power. Amen.

Joseph's Dream

Readings: Jer 23:5-8; Matt 1:18-25

Scripture:
> [T]he angel of the Lord appeared to [Joseph] in a dream
> and said, "Joseph, son of David,
> Do not be afraid to take Mary your wife into your home.
> For it is through the Holy Spirit
> that this child has been conceived in her" (Matt 1:20).

Reflection: Joseph knew that Mary was pregnant and that the child in her womb was not his. According to the Mosaic Law there was a written contract of marriage between them, a formal engagement. But Mary had not yet moved into Joseph's home, the culminating event of a Jewish marriage. Strictly speaking she could be stoned for this seeming infidelity. Joseph was in a real and agonizing bind. He, "a righteous man" (Matt 1:19) wanted to follow the law, but in his sensitivity and concern for Mary he could not bring himself to do her any harm. Finally he "decided to divorce her quietly" (Matt 1:19), that is, without making any public statement about his reasons.

What a time of inner turmoil and outer confusion and chaos it must have been for both of them. "Where are you God in all of this?" That would have been a normal question for two such faith-filled people. We can imagine that even after doing the best they could with their prayerful, reflective, rational decision-making, their hearts continued to reach out to God in cries deeper than words. And God did communicate with them at a level beyond words—through Joseph's dream.

When we are pulled apart on the horns of a dilemma, not finding any rational solutions to a problem, we can let the prayerful cries of our heart descend to that deeper level of our being which is beyond rational thought and words. After making the best choice we can in the light of reason, we can let go and trust God to help us in ways beyond our understanding. Then there can arise from that deeper intuitive level of our being a certitude and confidence which had previously escaped us. When, like Joseph, we make the best decision we can with an informed conscience, then let go trusting totally in God, the Divine Spirit can break through our confusion to enlighten our path and fill us with peace about our choice, even if it contradicts the social and religious patterns of our culture.

Meditation: What insoluble dilemmas have been or are a part of your life now? As your experience of trying to think your way to a solution fails, take some quiet time to let go gently of anxious thoughts repeating slowly a short phrase such as, "My soul rests in God alone . . ." (Psalm 62:2a).

Prayer: Mysterious Loving Presence, your ways are not our ways. We surrender to you the insoluble difficulties in which we are entangled. For the good of all concerned make us receptive to the guidance of your Holy Spirit. This we pray through Christ the source of your coming into our lives and world. Amen.

Great in God's Sight

Readings: Judg 13:2-7, 24-25a; Luke 1:5-25

Scripture:
Your wife Elizabeth will bear you a son,
  and you shall name him John.
And you will have joy and gladness,
  and many will rejoice at his birth,
    for he will be great in the sight of the Lord (Luke
    1:13b-15a).

Reflection: John the Baptist was not great in the world's eyes. Though his father was a priest and his mother was also from a priestly family, he himself did not follow that inherited vocation. Though in earlier centuries priests had enjoyed much prestige in Israel, by Zechariah's time they had little power or influence. When Herod became King of Judea about forty years before John's birth, he took over the appointment of the chief priest and limited him to a ceremonial role. In addition to their relatively humble status among their fellow citizens, Elizabeth and Zechariah, because of their childlessness, would have been thought of by their relatives, neighbors, and friends as cursed by God for some sinfulness of theirs.

John was the answer to his parents' prayer and the joy of their life. He was like them, a rural boy from the hill country who perhaps could have gained a little prestige or influence by following the traditional family vocation of priest. Instead he left home to live in the desert wearing animal skins and eating locusts and wild honey (Matt 3:4). He must have been a somewhat unusual fellow. However, his compelling lifestyle and prophetic voice captured the crowds who came out in droves to listen to him, respond to his call to repent, and be baptized by him (Luke 3:3-18).

John did not set his eyes or heart on wealth, power, or prestige. His eyes and heart were fixed on God. Because of that he recognized the Messiah and wanted only to decrease so that Christ might increase (John 3:30). In his poverty and humility he was great in God's sight. With a clear and insistent voice he cried out and continues to cry out to all of us to change our priorities and join in welcoming the reign of God in our midst. He invites us to let go our empty pursuit of riches, power, and prestige so that we may see Christ where he may be found— right in our midst in all the circumstances of daily life.

Meditation: Are there ways in which you are being invited to change your priorities so that greatness manifest in you will be greatness in God's sight?

Prayer: Great and loving Beginning and End of our lives, free us, as you will, from our excessive and compulsive efforts to achieve greatness in our own eyes and in the sight of others. Help us relax in your love and give ourselves over to prayer and work for your glory. We pray through the intercession of John the Baptist and all those who have gone before us in poverty and humility. Amen.

December 20: Wednesday of the Third Week of Advent

Nothing Impossible

Readings: Isa 7:10-14; Luke 1:26-38

Scripture:
But Mary said to the angel,
   "How can this be,
   since I have no relations with a man?"
And the angel said to her in reply,
   "The Holy Spirit will come upon you,
   and the power of the Most High will overshadow you.
   . . . . [N]othing will be impossible for God" (Luke 1:34-
   35a, 37a).

Reflection: Optimistic as we may be, we learn early in life that some things we desire are not possible. Bitter experiences teach life's limits.

In *Babette's Feast*, a story by Isak Dinesen made into a motion picture, Lorens Loewenhielm learns this. His deep attraction to Martine, one of the two beautiful daughters of a rigid pastor, goes unrequited because of her determination to devote her life to the "otherworldly" congregation. On his last visit to her home as a young man Lorens takes leave uttering in despair, "I have learned here . . . that in this world there are things which are impossible!" With wounded and hardened heart he sets out after wealth and glory.

Thirty years later Lorens, now a "successful" general, returns and becomes reconnected with the shriveled congregation. He accompanies his ancient aunt to the home of Martine and her sister Philippa to honor their deceased father. Their maid, Babette, has prepared a sumptuous feast. Worldly-wise Lorens recognizes and savors each dish and wine served. Transformed in spirit by the exquisite meal and the loving artistry and generosity with which it was prepared and served, he and the congregation are moved to a deeper level of love and forgiveness than any they had ever known. Lorens speaks movingly about the unconditional grace in which all the strands of life are reconciled. In this eucharistic gift he realizes the deep union in love that he has known and will know with Martine all her life. He says "[T]onight, I have learned . . . that in this world anything is possible."

Experiencing deep sorrow and disillusionment can never destroy the eternal reality in which all losses are made good. When God became human in the womb of Mary, divine love lavishly embraced all human experience making the one thing necessary possible: our loving union in Christ Jesus with God, the source of our lasting joy.

Meditation: Open to any bitterness and grief within you. Remember also ways you have known the goodness of life recalling that with God "no tear goes unheeded, no joy unnoticed" (Prayer for the Fifth Sunday in Ordinary Time).

Prayer: O God, you grant us joy to balance our affliction in this life. We pray that in Christ all our grief and joy will be transformed in the life to come. Amen.

December 21: Thursday of the Third Week of Advent

Leaping for Joy

Readings: Cant 2:8-14 or Zeph 3:14-18a; Luke 1:39-45

Scripture:
". . . [A]t the moment the sound of your greeting reached
   my ears,
   the infant in my womb leaped for joy" (Luke 1:44).

Reflection: Leaping for joy could easily be the theme of to-day's liturgy. In the first reading from the Song of Songs, the divine lover comes leaping over the hills (Cant 2:8). Mary's trip "to the hill country in haste" (Luke 1:39) might also be imagined as her leaping over the hills—an energetic and joyous venture of blessed reunion with her cousin Elizabeth celebrating God's great mercy and kindness manifest in both of them. When Mary bearing Jesus in her womb embraced her pregnant cousin Elizabeth, and the sound of her greeting reverberated in Elizabeth's ears, Elizabeth's child leaped for joy in her womb.

Athletes leap for joy when they score points, win games, cross the finish lines. Even casual viewers cannot but be caught up in the exuberant joy of such moments. Children jump for joy in happy response to pleasant surprises—the long-awaited and eagerly desired new toy for Christmas, the hoped for arrival of a much loved parent or grandparent. There is something about joy that cannot be contained in an earthbound body. Though felt and expressed with great enthusiasm, however, these joys are often experienced as fleeting. When the toy is broken, tears of grief tend to drown out the joy of the previous moment. When an anticipated celebration is over, a cloud of melancholy may overshadow joy. When the victory celebration ends and life is back to normal, a kind of depressed boredom at the humdrum may undermine any lasting joy.

Only realizing the divine presence as Mary, Elizabeth, and John did, brings us deep and lasting joy even in the midst of sorrow, loss, suffering and dying. The presence of Emmanuel, God-with-us, felt by Mary in her womb and by Elizabeth and John in the closeness of Mary's embrace and voice is the same presence of God in Christ who is coming into our lives in the Spirit of the risen Christ. The wonderful truth is that God is always present and loving us unconditionally in Christ. Receptivity to that reality can fill all our earthly joys with the infinite depth of lasting joy, and transform our sorrows with a joy no tears can wash away.

Meditation: Take some time to think about the things that bring you joy. Give thanks for the presence of God within them. Bring to mind what is causing you sadness. In faith ask God to open you to the joy and peace that lies within or beyond that.

Prayer: Spirit of God, you live within us always drawing us more deeply into Christ. Open us to that joy, which is the fruit of your presence. In Christ we pray this for ourselves and all our sisters and brothers. Amen.

December 22: Friday of the Third Week of Advent

Mercy

Readings: 1 Sam 24-28; Luke 1:46-56

Scripture:
"[God] has come to the help of his servant Israel
    for he remembered his promise of mercy . . . ." (Luke
    1:54).

Reflection: Three Hebrew words for mercy convey a richly
textured experience. One refers to the loving-kindness and
mutual accommodation of committed love between spouses
or friends. It is used also to describe the relationship between
God and Israel. Another is the plural form of "womb." Mercy
is a physically safe, loving, nurturing environment for
growth. A third Hebrew usage means "grace" or "favor."
Mercy gives freely—beyond expectation.

Though the God of the Hebrews is sometimes depicted as
wrathful toward evil, nevertheless, God's mercy and loving-
kindness trump every other image of the divine in both the
Old and New Testaments. The divine self-revelation in Exodus begins with God's expression of compassionate understanding of the people's suffering in Egypt, and the assertion
that he will rescue them (Exod 3:6-9). Over and over the
Psalmist cries out like this:

[Y]ou, Lord, are a merciful and gracious God,
    slow to anger, most loving and true" (Ps 86:15).

Even in the horrors of the exile the Isarelites knew that

> [t]he favors of the Lord are not exhausted,
>   his mercies are not spent (Lam 3:22).

God's mercy in human history breaks through in its fullness in Jesus whose mission was to heal and save. He came not only for the healthy and righteous, but especially for the sick and sinners. His word and life proclaimed the compassionate reign of God's merciful love present in our world.

In today's gospel reading, Mary rejoices that the mercy of God is with us in the child growing in her womb. God, whose compassionate desire is to save the poor, the oppressed, the needy and the sinner, becomes human in one who is herself lowly, poor, a servant. Divine mercy in Jesus continues to come into our lives through his Spirit in our own lowliness. He stands with us in our weakness and need, sits at our table and shares what we have, stays with us in our lives just as they are. Graciously accepting and rejoicing in that mercy now is our best way of preparing to welcome it in Christ's glorious coming at the end of our lives and of time.

Meditation: In what ways do you need mercy? With trust open to that mercy in Christ who lives within you. Today open your heart in mercy to those you meet, hear, read, and think about.

Prayer: Infinite Mercy, you have become human and continue to live in us in Christ. Flooded with awareness of your merciful love may we be merciful to our sisters and brothers. We pray this in Christ our merciful brother. Amen.

December 23: Saturday of the Third Week of Advent

Zechariah and Elizabeth

Readings: Mal 3:1-4, 23-24; Luke 1:57-66

Scripture:
When they came on the eighth day to circumcise the child,
    they were going to call him Zechariah after his father,
    but his mother said in reply,
    "No. He will be called John" (Luke 1:59-60).

Reflection: The name "John" means "God is gracious." John the Baptist's name comes out of nine months of silence his father Zechariah experienced when he was unable to accept God's work in his life. Zechariah was struck dumb when he doubted Gabriel's message that his wife Elizabeth would bear a son (Luke 1:12-20). At the time of the child's circumcision, Zechariah needed the power of Elizabeth's speech to say "He will be called John" (Luke 1:60). Naming the child John was itself a striking departure from the Israelite tradition of giving the first son the name of his grandfather. Elizabeth's necessary role as the one who spoke the name during the rite of circumcision because of Zechariah's muteness was also a startling change from the custom of having the father announce the name. Breaking the silence when she names the child who had been growing in the silence of her womb, Elizabeth is the first to manifest to the world the truth of God's graciousness embodied in John.

Whether women or men we all have an interior Zechariah and an interior Elizabeth. When our masculine, rational Zechariah is struck dumb and we are speechless, however that happens—whether through doubt or through sorrow, ecstatic joy, fatigue, the inner turmoil of creativity, sickness, failure, or success—the Spirit of God works in us at a more interior level of our being. In silence from our inner Elizabeth, a deep intuitive place beyond rational knowing and previous experience, the gracious presence of God rises up and speaks. We are invited to trust in the divine graciousness at work in our lives in that place beyond our capacity to understand immediately or to articulate at once. What God brings to birth and articulates through our Elizabeths will be affirmed by our Zechariahs: "His name is John," that is, "God is gracious."

Meditation: Recall an event in your life that left you speechless or brought you to a deep silence that eventually led you to a greater understanding and naming of God's graciousness.

Prayer: God of Elizabeth, Zechariah, and John, be with us when we are unable to speak, opening us in silence to your divine graciousness. Out of that silence help us to speak your goodness in our world in a new way. This we pray in the gracious Spirit of Christ Jesus, in whom we live. Amen.

FOURTH WEEK OF ADVENT

Hope

Readings: Mic 5:1-4a; Heb 10:5-10; Luke 1:39-45

Scripture:
[A]nd Elizabeth, filled with the Holy Spirit,
cried out in a loud voice and said,
"Blessed are you among women,
And blessed is the fruit of your womb. . . .
For at the moment the sound of your greeting reached my
ears,
the infant in my womb leaped for joy" (Luke 1:41b-42, 44).

Reflection: Hope is the spark in every human soul that keeps us longing and waiting patiently for something good to come. We hope for lots of specific good things—a great vacation, acceptance into graduate school, a raise at work, recovering from an illness, winning the lottery, the safe birth of a baby. Hope is also a theological virtue, an essential part of our baptismal life in God and God's life in us. It gives us the capacity to keep the inner eye of our hearts and the energy of our lives open to the indeterminate, unknown and surprising ways the divine reign comes into our lives today and the ways it will come in glory at the end of time.

The hope of Advent comes to fullness in the pregnancies of Elizabeth with John and Mary with Jesus. Pregnancy is a wonderful symbol for hope. Pregnant parents and their other children hope for a healthy, beautiful little child to become a part of their circle of love. It is a time of joyful expectation. It also has its dark side. Pregnancies bring morning sickness, fatigue, and mood swings for mothers. Fathers worry about changing relationships and new responsibilities. Siblings may feel jealous, unsure of their places.

The child in the womb, the source of hope, is also surrounded by darkness. In a normal pregnancy this darkness is not threatening, but rather secure, comforting, and nourishing. Though a time of unknowing and unseeing it is a time of living in absolute trust in the loving mother-father life nourishing and cherishing it.

Just as Mary was pregnant with the child Jesus, so we and our earth are pregnant with the reign of God in Christ growing within us. God is also pregnant with us, transforming the human community and our earth into the body of Christ which will come to birth in the fullness of time. Advent celebrates the hope these pregnancies bring.

Meditation: Stirring up the theological hope that lives in you, find ways to express your trust that the reign of God is growing silently and mysteriously in our darkness.

Prayer: Life-giving, nurturing God, you filled Elizabeth and Mary with hope and expectation during their pregnancies. Stir up your gift of hope in us as we look for the ways God continues to bring our world to birth. Fill us with confidence in you as we labor to give birth to Christ in our world. We pray in Jesus' name. Amen.

December 24: Sunday of the Fourth Week of Advent   **51**

CHRISTMAS AND DAYS
WITHIN ITS OCTAVE

December 25: Solemnity of Christmas

Vigil Mass: Genealogy

Readings: Isa 62:1-5; Acts 13:16-17, 22-25; Matt 1:1-25 or Matt 1:18-25

Scripture:
The book of the genealogy of Jesus Christ,
   The son of David, the son of Abraham (Matt 1:1).

Reflection: Many experience this long genealogy as the dullest reading of the year. What do its foreign sounding names have to do with us? And it seems too focused on "the fathers," even though a few "mothers" are included.

Listening to my two older sisters and my brother-in-law rehearse family ancestry and connections with friends, neighbors, or acquaintances that lived in our hometown for any length of time used to amaze me. I could never keep them all straight. Yet, just listening to the recital gave me a sense of being rooted in this place in the world with these people, my deepest memories forever immersed in that part of the earth. Ruminating over pictures, old news releases and birth, baptismal, and marriage certificates, part of the work some cousins have done on our maternal grandfather's ancestry, also helped us know who we are. Maybe that is why I don't mind hearing this list.

As we let Matthew's genealogy wash over us, we absorb the reality of God's becoming human like us in the particular place in time and history prepared for him through his ancestry with all its illustrious, notorious, and obscure characters and events. The patriarchal nature of the culture he was born into—and in which we continue to live—may emphasize his male ancestors, but his human link with us comes through his mother and his many grandmothers, named and unnamed, as well as through his grandfathers. In Jesus, God has come to be one with us in our humanity in all the particularities of our history and our experience.

Meditation: Name some of your grandmothers and grandfathers, old neighbors and friends who are an important part of your identity. Thank God for coming into human history in Jesus through his unique ancestry and living in you through your particular lineage and place in the world.

Prayer: God-with-us in the humanity of Jesus, we live in awe and wonder in the mystery of your love. Enlighten our minds and warm our hearts to all the particular ways you have been and are with us in our families and neighborhoods. This we pray in you Jesus, Emmanuel. Amen.

Mass at Midnight: Outcasts and Strangers

Readings: Isa 9:1-6; Titus 2:11-14; Luke 2:1-14

Scripture:
While they were there,
   the time came for her to have her child,
   and she gave birth to her firstborn son.
She wrapped him in swaddling clothes and laid him in a
      manger,
   because there was no room for them in the inn (Luke
      2:6-7).

Reflection: "[T]here was no room for them" (Luke 2:7) What a poignant phrase. There are many in our cities and our world today for whom there is no room: the growing numbers of homeless, thousands who are fleeing from oppressive governments, abandoned children, those displaced by hurricanes and earthquakes. To many of us they are often all but invisible. They rise like an occasional blip in the headlines while their pictures and stories are brought momentarily to our attention and then quickly drop away. Most of us have not been homeless, displaced, or exiled so we do not know what it is like not to have the basic physical necessities of life—a clean and warm place to sleep, a bathroom, water and supplies for personal hygiene, and safe food to eat. The homeless and displaced often lack also the love and support of others necessary for survival. Being passed by day after day, sometimes as dangerous, and often as if they did not exist, takes a devastating toll on their sense of worth. There are too those who in old age have been uprooted to move to homes for the elderly. No matter how competent and sensitive the care, the person needing to be there may constantly know the ache of wanting to go home.

Whether or not we have ever been without a home, there is a kind of homelessness that is a part of every life. It is an inner experience, a homelessness of heart that nags at our souls sometimes even in the midst of the warmth of family or friends by whom we are loved and with whom we feel a sense of belonging. Though the earth and our particular place on earth as well as our loved ones do truly provide a home where we belong now, still our human hearts long for our eternal home.

In Jesus God came to share our temporary home on earth. In his identification with the stranger, the outcast, and the homeless from the beginning of his earthly life he assures all of us that like him, and with and in him, we will find our lasting home in God.

Meditation: Call to mind some of the homeless people around you and in other parts of the world. Be aware of ways in which you feel out of place, restless or not at home. With faith in God with us in Christ Jesus, entrust them and yourself to him as our lasting home.

Prayer: Loving God, you are our eternal home. We give thanks for your coming in Jesus to share our home on earth so that we may live forever in you. We pray this in Jesus' name. Amen.

Mass at Dawn: A New Day

Readings: Isa 62:11-12; Titus 3:4-7; Luke 2:15-20

Scripture:
When the angels went away from them to heaven,
  the shepherds said to one another,
  "Let us go, then, to Bethlehem
  to see this thing that has taken place,
  which the Lord has made known to us" (Luke 2:15).

Reflection: There are times when we go to bed heavy hearted about some insoluble problem, some trouble too heavy to bear. We are too fatigued to think or to do anything about it, even to pray consciously. We can only entrust ourselves to God in sleep. Waking the next morning as the first rays of light spill over the horizon we sense a new spirit within us. Though we still may not know what to do, our joy in life is renewed. We feel the energy of a new day, a new world, a chance to give it all another go, even with no certainty about how things will work out. Dawn brings Julian of Norwich's sense that "all shall be well, and all manner of things shall be well!"

Dawn on the morning of Christ's birth, I suspect, arrived in Bethlehem just as quietly and usual as any other—the first barely perceptible glow of the sun just over the horizon followed by the silent, gradual spread of its radiance and rose-pink fingers into the morning sky. Only Mary, Joseph, and the shepherds knew "this thing that has taken place, which the Lord has made known to us" (Luke 2:15b).

But this quiet dawn illumined the great mystery of the new creation which was for all people. Through incarnation in the humanity of Jesus, God brought to completion the union of the divinity with the stuff of humanity, the earth and the entire created world—rocks and roots, stars and planets, soil and sap, water and blood, hearts and hands. God who was and is always present in creation had come to be born, live, grow, suffer, and die like us and with us here on earth. God in Jesus was not here to stay for a time and then leave us, but to remain with us always in the Spirit of the resurrected Christ, the internal energy of our living, dying, rising. Just as creation begins its "first day" with dawn when the Spirit of God broods over the darkness of chaos and says "Let there be light" (Gen 1:3), so it reaches the first day of its fullness at the dawn of Christ's birth. Today we celebrate that dawn.

Meditation: If you are up at dawn, sit in the dark and watch the new day emerge. Rejoice in the dawn of the new creation in Jesus Christ who is rising as the sun in you and all of creation.

Prayer: Jesus, you are the dawn of our new day. Open us as you will and as we are able to the new life, light, and love rising in our hearts and world through the energy of your life within us. We pray in your name. Amen.

Mass During the Day: A Good Word

Readings: Isa 52:7-10; Heb 1:1-6; John 1:1-18

Scripture:
And the Word became flesh
and made his dwelling among us,
and we saw his glory,
the glory as of the Father's only Son,
full of grace and truth (John 1:14).

Reflection: "Sticks and stones may break my bones, but words can never hurt me." I do not know the origin of this chant, one we probably all learned in childhood. Using it to tell another kid that we were not affected by her or his mean words was a way we tried to say they had no power over us. The truth was more likely that their words did wound us and diminish our trust in our goodness. Words have a lot of power. Thoughtless, insensitive, angry, manipulative, controlling, insulting, degrading, abusive words can destroy another's spirit and diminish their bodily well-being. Good words foster the growth of self-confidence, trust, and love with all the joy and peace that brings.

God has been speaking for a long time—good words. Whenever God spoke, something good happened: creation, freedom for the people of God through their Exodus out of Egypt, and guidance through the prophets. "In times past," the Letter to the Hebrews tells us, "God spoke in partial and various ways

/ to our ancestors through the prophets . . ." (Heb 1:1). Sometimes God's words, especially through the prophets, were challenging—not because of any intention to harm, but because God knew we were good and could do better, be more kind and loving to others, more inclusive, more just.

All God's effective words are partial expressions of the one Word God utters with such divine power that it embodies the fullness of God's life and goodness: "the Word who was with God . . . in the beginning" (John 1:1), and through whom "all things came to be" (John 1:3). In Jesus, the Christ, the Messiah, this "Word became flesh / and made his dwelling among us" (John 1:14). United in Christ, a reality we Christians first celebrate in baptism, we continue every moment to receive God's fullness in our lives in and through him (John 1:16). Our words are meant to echo, expand, highlight and convey to one another the infinite goodness and kindness of that one Word. Then our walking sensitively and surely upon the mountains of life will be beautiful and effective as we bring the good news of salvation and peace—that the God who is good reigns in our lives (Isa 52:7).

Meditation: Welcome the Word of God in your heart and mind. Ask for that Word to transform your every thought and word with goodness and kindness.

Prayer: Welcome, Word of God made flesh in Jesus. Through the power of your Spirit make our thoughts and words expressions of the good news you came to bring—that the reign of God who is love is here with us in you. Amen.

December 26: Feast of St. Stephen, First Martyr

Witness of Love

Readings: Acts 6:8-10; 7:54-59; Matt 10:17-22

Scripture:
Jesus said to his disciples:
"When they hand you over,
   do not worry about how you are to speak
   or what you are to say.
You will be given at that moment what you are to say.
For it will not be you who speak
   but the Spirit of your Father speaking through you"
      (Matt 10:19-20).

Reflection: By the time Matthew wrote, the early Christian community was facing persecution and martyrdom because of their witness to the Good News. In today's gospel passage, written as all the gospels are from the post-resurrection perspective, the risen Christ reassures them and us not to worry about what we will say when challenges to our witness to God's reign come. It is the Spirit of God who will speak through us. Divine love living in us will prevail. Stephen, the first martyr, had this experience.

Filled with grace Stephen had been doing wonderful things among the people (Acts 6:8). Though these wonders are not named, it seems they must have had some connection with his humble service—that table service the first deacons were appointed for so the Twelve could preach the word of God (Acts 6:2-5). Some people were upset by these wonders and signs and engaged Stephen in debate. He did not back down, but witnessed powerfully to Jesus as the fulfillment of Moses, the Law, and the Temple. Those who had been upset by his wonder-working were infuriated by this teaching which did not fit in to their understanding and expectations (Acts 7:54).

Stephen—totally given to a life of humble, loving service—manifested in word and deed the wonders of divine love incarnate in Jesus. His challenging message and his embodiment of it in his person were rejected. That rejection, however, did not quench the love of God, the Spirit of Christ within him. He spoke the truth courageously, even in the face of death, never departing from the way of love—love for Christ, and inclusive and forgiving love of his opponents. His last words were like those of Jesus on the cross, "Lord Jesus, receive my spirit," and "Lord, do not hold this sin against them" (Acts 7:59-60; cf. Luke 23:46, 34).

Meditation: Think about situations in your life that may require you to speak the truth in love. Let go for now worrying about what you will say, and choose to trust the Spirit of God who will work in you.

Prayer: Gracious God, you who are love speak that love in your Word. Through the power of your Spirit guide our words so that they may convey your truth in love. We pray through and in you, Jesus Christ, Word made flesh. Amen.

December 27: Feast of St. John, Apostle and Evangelist

Love's Sensitivity

Readings: 1 John 1:1-4; John 20:1a, 2-8

Scripture:
[Simon Peter and the other disciple whom Jesus loved]
both ran, but the other disciple ran faster than Peter
  and arrived at the tomb first;
    he bent down and saw the burial cloths there, but did
      not go in.
  When Simon Peter arrived after him,
    he went into the tomb. . . .
Then the other disciple also went in. . . . (John 20:4-8).

Reflection: Christian tradition identifies John as the "Beloved Disciple," the one who at the last supper sat next to Jesus, close enough physically and intimate enough in relationship to lean back and rest his head on Jesus' chest while reclining at table.

Love is among the key perspectives of the fourth gospel. Early on that oft quoted verse—"For God so loved the world that he gave his only Son, so that everyone who believes in him might not perish but might have eternal life" (John 3:16)—assures us of God's love for us. Jesus' last discourse to his disciples—chapters 14 through 17—conveys to us the intimate, unifying love of God that the Advocate, the Spirit pours out in us through Jesus' death and rising in glory. "On that day," Jesus says, "you will realize that I am in my Father and you are in me and I in you" (John 14:20). What closer, greater love is possible? Now we, "the branches," live in Christ, "the vine" (John 15:5). This love is not abstract or heady. Jesus demonstrated that by his intimacy with his friends, and by humble service, washing the feet of his disciples (John 13), giving up his life for them and us.

In today's gospel John shows us that the greatest love is manifested in little things—daily sensitivities to others' feelings. The time of the death of a loved one can arouse competition among the close survivors about who was most loved. When arriving at Jesus' tomb John stepped aside so Peter could enter first. Knowing personally the deep unconditional love of God frees us to be sensitive to the feelings of others. Great love reaches out through the smallest things—stepping aside so someone else can be first.

Meditation: Open your heart to the great love God has for you. Rest in it. Think of some small gesture or action that may convey that love in unobtrusive sensitivity to a family member, friend, or casual acquaintance.

Prayer: Great God of infinite love, our lives are made up of many small things. Help us open to ways we can manifest your great love in ordinary, little ways. We pray this in Jesus whose love for John, Peter, and Mary Magdalene transformed their lives in love. Amen.

December 28: Feast of the Holy Innocents, Martyrs

The Power of Love

Readings: 1 John 1:5–2:2; Matt 2:13-18

Scripture:
When the magi had departed, behold,
  the angel of the Lord appeared to Joseph in a dream and
    said,
  "Rise, take the child and his mother, flee to Egypt,
  And stay there until I tell you.
Herod is going to search for the child to destroy him"
  (Matt 2:13).

Reflection: Get up, flee, your child is in mortal danger. Jarred from sleep by this angelic warning in a dream, Joseph with Mary set out in haste to find sanctuary for Jesus—in exile, in a foreign land. Weary and frightened as they might have been, they summoned up the courage they needed to protect Jesus from the brutality of Herod's insatiable thirst for domineering power, an experience familiar to many people in our world. Abused wives and children, innocent victims of ethnic, religious and political oppression can readily identify. Some make it to safety—for now; others, like the Holy Innocents, suffer violent death at the hands of merciless killers. The human struggle for domination over others, and our unflinching will to use violence to achieve it continues.

Jesus was not after anybody's earthly throne, nor was he about controlling anyone's life. He came to reveal the power of divine Love which, as Saint Paul tells us, works effectively in kindness, patience, courtesy, humility. It does not seek its own, but others' good fortune (1 Cor 13:4-7). That power, as Jesus demonstrated by his life, manifests itself in compassion and service. It seeks out and encourages the poor, the sick, the sinner. It promotes justice, peace and goodness. Whereas the power of domination that lived in Herod quakes in the face of threat and grows more paranoid, the power of love casts out fear (1 John 4:18). It has the courage to risk flight for the good of another and, as Jesus' death and resurrection demonstrate, it can also stand firm with dignity in the face of unavoidable violence, believing that God's love will prevail.

Divine love lives in us. Overcoming our fear it fills us with courage to flee for our true good and the good of others when we must, and to stand firm when necessary.

Meditation: Recall those who are fleeing oppression and abuse today and those who are helping them. Recall also those who are undergoing torture and death. Pray that they may experience the strength of God's love.

Prayer: Lover of the poor and oppressed, your infinite compassion embraces in love distraught exiles, abused children and suffering families. Give them the strength and consolation they need, and help us find ways to support and free them. We pray in Jesus' name. Amen.

December 29: The Fifth Day in the Octave of Christmas

The Light of Love

Readings: 1 John 2:3-11; Luke 2:22-35

Scripture:
[Simeon] blessed God, saying:
"Lord, now let your servant go in peace;
   your word has been fulfilled:
my own eyes have seen the salvation
   which you prepared in the sight of every people,
a light to reveal you to the nations
   and the glory of your people Israel" (Luke 2: 28b-32).

Reflection: When the long dark nights of winter are followed by days of clouds and fog, even the sunniest dispositions droop. Not only our ability to see, but our moods are affected. Full-spectrum lighting, the kind closely resembling natural light, becomes very important for some. Studies have shown that some children deprived of such light are afflicted not only by irritability and depression, but by attention deficit disorder. By the third or fourth day of no sunshine I find myself lingering over ads for full-spectrum lighting!

In the first letter of John the author asserts that "God is light, and in [God] there is no darkness at all" (1 John 1:5b). Walking in that light is about love, whereas living in hate is living in darkness (1 John 2:9-11). In one of the great "I am" statements pointing to his divinity, Jesus says, "I am the Light of the world" (John 8:12). Simeon sees and proclaims that divine Light when Mary and Joseph present Jesus in the temple (Luke 2:32).

The light of God in Christ is our full-spectrum spiritual light. Its presence in us was revealed in our baptism. It continues to douse the darkness of hatred and bring us into a loving relationship with God and others. This light of Love, the Spirit of God in Christ, radiates within us and all creation. It provides the ambience for our seeing more and more clearly what is good in ourselves, others, and our world, and illumines what is destructive. It provides the warmth and energy needed to affirm and develop that good, and to resist the evil without falling into the destructive ways of violence and hatred. No matter how dark our winters, we are able to walk securely and energetically in the light of Christ.

Meditation: Take some time to sit quietly and get in touch with the places of darkness within and around you—feelings of fear, hatred, distress, conflicted relationships, unjust systems and structures. Welcome them and with trust open them to transformation in the light of Christ.

Prayer: Christ Jesus, you are the light of the world. Open the eyes of our minds and hearts to the ways you are shining in our darkness. This we pray in your Spirit. Amen.

Widows

Readings: 1 John 2:12-17; Luke 2:36-40

Scripture:
There was a prophetess, Anna,
> the daughter of Phanuel, of the tribe of Asher.

She was advanced in years,
> having lived seven years with her husband after her
> marriage,
> and then as a widow until she was eighty-four.

She never left the temple,
> but worshiped night and day with fasting and prayer
> (Luke 2:36-37).

Reflection: Widows and widowers know the wrenching grief the death of a spouse brings, and the great gaping wound it leaves in one's life. Anna, the prophetess, experienced this at much too young an age. She could not have been much older than twenty-one or twenty-two, a widow for over sixty years. In a culture where a woman's identity was essentially connected to her relationship with her father or husband being thrust into this state must have been particularly devastating. Deep grief, no matter what its source, has a way of shaking the foundations of our identity. Who are we when we are no longer someone's wife, husband, child, parent, friend? When we are no longer secretary, lawyer, teacher, cook? When we can no longer garden, walk, see?

Primitive societies allowed a widow communally protected solitary space to mourn her loss, accept her vulnerability, and reach within for a renewed and deepened identity. Anna found that protected space in the Temple. There she was able to find her identity in God. Healed and renewed she became a spokesperson for God, a prophet.

Our losses can be openings to a deeper identity. If with the support of others we allow ourselves the protected solitary time and space needed to turn more totally to God accepting, adjusting to, and integrating our losses in life, those unnerving psychic earthquakes can deepen our experience and conviction of God's ever-loving presence. In the light of that presence we see in new ways, and we are able to reveal God's compassionate presence to others.

Meditation: Think about some loss you have experienced and the healing made possible by time for solitude and prayer supported by friends, family, or community. Express your gratitude to God. Bring to mind with compassion someone you know who is going through a similar experience.

Prayer: Compassionate God, you transformed Anna through a life of solitude and prayer. In the loneliness of our losses draw us more deeply into your love so we may see you more clearly and respond to you more sensitively in others. Amen.

DECEMBER 31–JANUARY 6

December 31: Feast of the Holy Family
(Catholic Church)

The Seventh Day in the Octave of Christmas
(Episcopal Church)

Living with Others

Readings: Sir 3:2-7, 12-14 or 1 Sam 1:20-22, 24-28; Col 3:12-21 or 3:12-17 or 1 John 3:1-2, 21-14; Luke 2:41-52

Scripture:
[H]is mother said to him,
  "Son, why have you done this to us?
Your father and I have been looking for you with great
    anxiety."
And he said to them,
  "Why were you looking for me?
Did you not know that I must be in my Father's house?"
  (Luke 2:48-49).

Reflection: Human like us in every respect, Jesus' growth through adolescence would have been similar to ours. Struggling with the question "Who am I?" would have been a major issue for him at this time in his life. From his perspective the decision to try out his identity as divine teacher through dialogue with the elders in the temple would be appropriate and compelling. Though we cannot know his reasons for going ahead without informing his parents, his failure to do so surely gave Mary and Joseph a scare. His mother's response when he is found is direct and honest: What were you thinking! We were so worried about you! Jesus is equally honest: Can't you understand that I needed to do this? That this choice had to do with who I am?

Not only raising a child or being a child in a family, but living as adults in families and communities with others we cannot fully understand, is a challenging vocation. Sometimes it is baffling and anxiety-producing. The path to mutual loving acceptance has its rough spots. Today's gospel gives us some insights about dealing with these in ways that foster our growth as the unique manifestations God wishes each to be in our world: respectfully and honestly owning and expressing our perceptions and feelings about ourselves and the way another's behavior affects us; staying open and accepting of the other even when we do not understand; cultivating the flexibility and generosity to adjust our behavior and responses to the legitimate needs and expectations of others.

Meditation: Think of some challenging relationship in which you are engaged. What would you like honestly to say to the other person? Are you willing to hear what the other has to say? Let go and entrust all to God.

Prayer: Jesus, your family life with Mary and Joseph had challenges like the ones we experience in family and community. Help us be respectfully and sensitively open and honest with each other, while adjusting to others' needs in ways that promote true harmony and peace. Amen.

January 1: Solemnity of Mary, Mother of God
(Catholic Church)

The Holy Name
(Episcopal Church)

Silent Reflection

Readings: Num 6:22-27; Gal 4:4-7; Luke 2:16-21

Scripture:
All who heard it were amazed
    by what had been told them by the shepherds.
And Mary kept all these things,
    reflecting on them in her heart (Luke 2:18-19).

Reflection: When Mary heard the shepherds exclaiming how the angels had proclaimed her child the Messiah, and when she saw the amazement of those listening to the shepherds, she didn't immediately phone her neighbors or call the local newspapers and TV stations to let them know about her wonderful child and all the great things he would do. She "kept all these things, reflecting on them in her heart" (Luke 2:19). Out of the depths of her silent reflection came the light to grow into a deeper understanding of her son and ultimately the courage to stand by him in his mission as the suffering Messiah (John 19:25-27).

Sharing good news is important, but silence before speaking makes it possible for the Spirit within to clarify our thoughts and feelings. In our fast-paced world silence does not often come naturally. The rate at which visual images confront us, the number of words we hear per minute on radio and television, the sheer volume of e-mail and voice messages that besiege us daily, the insistent beat of much contemporary music—all these tend to ratchet up our inner pulse and increase our drive to keep things moving in anxious chatter and quick responses. The atmosphere around us does not encourage silent reflective pauses.

Yet there is a level of understanding in us which lies deeper than facile, upper level rational thought and immediate off-the-cuff responses. This is a level deeper than knee-jerk reactions to people and events that come out of habitual attitudes. This is the level of heart—the interior, secret core of our being where we dwell in Christ secure in the divine love. In this secret place the reign of God is alive and active. Taking the time as Mary did to let the words and events of life sink into that secret, quiet place makes it possible for us at the appropriate time to speak out and act confidently in ways that effectively express and promote God's reign of love.

Meditation: Sit quietly for twenty or thirty minutes. Attend to your breath. Don't control it, just observe it. If a prayer phrase rises within you, repeat it slowly; breathe naturally. Rest.

Prayer: Gracious God, you are the Mystery of life that slumbers within all of us. Give us the kind of trust and courage Mary had, so that we can let you draw us into the silence of your presence. We pray in Christ your Son. Amen.

January 2

Being "Somebody"

Readings: 1 John 2:22-28; John 1:19-28

Scripture:
So they said to [John],
   "Who are you, so we can give an answer to those who
      sent us?
What do you have to say for yourself?"
He said:
   "I am *the voice of one crying out in the desert,
   'Make straight the way of the Lord,'*
   as Isaiah the prophet said" (John 1:22-23).

Reflection: Most of us want to be somebody, at least in some modest way. We'd like an identity that impresses someone. A cartoon shared by a friend some time ago captured this reality in a way that most of us can laugh at—at least when we have become more conscious of our futile drives for recognition! A person with a dismayed look on his face was saying to a friend: "Well I always knew I wanted to be somebody; now I know I should have been more specific!" In today's gospel John the Baptist presents an arresting contrast to our exaggerated drives for self-identity.

The truth, of course, is that each of us is somebody. But our unique identity is not one we have frantically to carve out for ourselves at the expense of others, or even of our own health, by driving hard, defeating others, and climbing to the top. That is the usual approach we take because we come to full self-consciousness without realizing we are unconditionally loved by God and connected to others in love.

The path to our true identity as a unique child of God, the voice God wants us to be, is the one taken by John. It does not mean abandoning all efforts to develop our talents. Like John, however, we can with God's help let go anxious thoughts about ourselves and the impressions we make on others. Our deep and unshakeable foundation is in God living in us. That divine life is at the core of our identity—the Word lives in us. Like John, if we drop our compulsive drives to make a self according to our own image and welcome the image of God which we are, we also become a voice that gives unique shape to the Word of God.

Meditation: Allow yourself to be aware of anxieties you might have about yourself. Entrust them to God; repeat slowly, "As you will, give voice to your Word in me." Let the phrase simplify. When you are drawn, rest in trust.

Prayer: Word of God, you are the sure foundation of our lives. Help us open to the unique way you wish to speak in our lives so that together we may rejoice in you. We pray through the power of your Spirit within us. Amen.

Justice

Readings: 1 John 2:29–3:6; John 1:29-34

Scripture:
John the Baptist saw Jesus coming toward him and said,
   "Behold, the Lamb of God, who takes away the sin of
      the world. . . .
I did not know him,
   but the one who sent me to baptize with water told me,
   'On whomever you see the Spirit come down and
      remain,
   he is the one who will baptize with the Holy Spirit'"
      (John 1:29, 33).

Reflection: At a prayer breakfast in Washington, D.C. in early February, 2006, U2 rock star Bono spoke movingly of our call as human beings of all faiths to work for justice and equality. There is one thing, he said, that all of us of every faith and ideology can agree on: ". . . that God is with the vulnerable and poor." He goes on:

> God is in the slums, in the cardboard boxes where the poor play house. God is in the silence of a mother who has infected her child with a virus that will end both their lives. God is in the cries heard under the rubble of war. God is in the debris of wasted opportunity and lives, and God is with us if we are with them.

This God who is with the vulnerable and poor is with us in the Lamb of God whom John the Baptist points out to us today. John would have been aware of that title used for Isaiah's Suffering Servant who would "bring forth justice to the nations . . ." (Isa 52:13–53:12 and Isa 42:1b; 42:6a). Jesus, the Lamb of God, is that Suffering Servant. In him God suffers with the poor and oppressed in order to bring all people and all nations to freedom and justice.

At the end of today's gospel passage John tells us that this Servant on whom the Spirit rests "'is the one who will baptize [us] with the Holy Spirit'" (John 1:34). Through baptism the same Spirit who lives in Jesus as servant lives in us, drawing us into his identity and into his mission for justice. In him the divine light will shine out and new life for our suffering world will bubble up from within and among us like a never-failing spring of fresh life-giving water (Isa 58:6-11).

Meditation: Who are the poor in your community, your neighborhood, city and state? During your time of prayer invite them in imagination into your presence seeing and honoring God's presence in them. Are there ways you are called to be with them?

Prayer: Jesus, you who suffer in the poor and afflicted, open our eyes and hearts to your presence in those unjustly treated in our world. Fill us with compassion and energy to reach out to them and to work for justice. This we pray, trusting in your Spirit who lives within us. Amen.

Stop, Look, and Listen

Readings: 1 John 3:7-10; John 1:35-42

Scripture:
John was standing with two of his disciples,
   and as he watched Jesus walk by, he said,
   "Behold, the Lamb of God."
The two disciples heard what he said and followed Jesus
   (John 1:35-37).

Reflection: Because John was standing there with two of his disciples and watching he noticed Jesus walk by and recognized him as the Messiah. Because the two disciples who were standing there with John were listening, they heard what he said and knew what he meant: Follow him, not me! They set out after Jesus. Jesus was aware of them. He responded to their eagerness and invited them to spend the day with him. Because one of those disciples, Andrew, knew his brother Simon would also be interested, he brought him along.

The beginning of a lifelong process of transformation for these disciples of Jesus had its humble beginnings on a seemingly ordinary day. They might have missed their opportunity if they had not been content to stand there with John watching and listening. Things might have been different if they had not, after hearing John, had the light and courage to follow Jesus and enter into conversation with him.

If we are too busy doing things to take time to stand still and watch, we may not notice that Jesus is passing by. We may not hear those pointing out his presence. In order to be spiritually alert we have to be willing to stop, look, and listen. Unless we do, and unless we are willing to risk changing our course, we may miss opportunities to follow and converse with Jesus. We may not hear him saying, "Come, and you will see" (John 1:39). We may miss a chance to stay with him and to bring others to him.

Jesus, however, never walks out of our lives. He is always aware of us, waiting for us to become aware of him. He is always inviting us to follow and stay with him. Every ordinary day is an opportune time to "stop, look, and listen" for his loving presence.

Meditation: Choose several times today not to do immediately the next thing you had planned to do. Instead, stop for a minute or five to look and listen in an unhurried way at what is going on within and around you. Notice what you feel, see, or hear. Then decide what to do next.

Prayer: Jesus, you are always with us. Inspired by your Spirit help us set aside any narrow-sighted plans and excessive activity that keep us from being aware of your loving companionship and guidance in the events of our daily lives. We pray with trust in you. Amen.

Son of Man

Readings: 1 John 3:11-21; John 1:43-51

Scripture:
Jesus answered and said to [Nathanael],
  "Do you believe
  because I told you that I saw you under the fig tree?
You will see greater things than this."
And he said to him, "Amen, amen, I say to you,
  you will see the sky opened and the angels of God
  ascending and descending on the Son of Man" (John
    1:49-51).

Reflection: Once when visiting my sister-in-law and brother, their youngest daughter, about four, had the flu. She was crying, "But I don't want to be sick!" Life teaches us that some sickness is an inevitable part of being human. Not only do we not like some parts of being human, we tend to think that becoming more open to God requires leaving our humanity behind. In fatigue, temptation, failure, and suffering we are apt to feel that God is absent. Jesus' life, however, demonstrates that the divine presence permeates and brings eternal life through these experiences as well as through experiences of strength, health, and success.

The phrase 'son of man' in today's gospel is often associated with the apocalyptic figure described in the book of

Daniel: "One like a son of man coming, on the clouds of heaven; . . . [who] received dominion, glory, and kingship; nations and peoples of every language serve him" (Dan 7:13b, 14a). If Jesus was using it in that way he would be identifying himself the triumphant Messiah who would come at the end of the ages. But in Hebrew the term "son of man" often simply meant a human being. Jesus is the triumphant Messiah who will come at the end of time, but his way to that end leads through all the experiences of being human. In him we are invited, as Saint Paul says, to have this "same attitude that is also [ours] in Christ Jesus,

> Who, though he was in the form of God,
> did not regard equality with God something
>   to be grasped.
> Rather, he emptied himself, . . .
> coming in human likeness . . ." (Phil 2:6-7a, c).

Meditation: Take time to focus on the joys and challenges of being human at your stage in life. Note what you resist and what you easily welcome. Pick one experience of each. Welcome both trusting Christ in them.

Prayer: Christ Jesus, though we often resist our humanity, you freely embraced our joys and our weakness. Grace us with that same attitude so that we may not miss the transforming presence of your Spirit in all the experiences of our lives. This we pray with gratitude for your becoming one of us and living in us now through your Spirit. Amen.

January 6
(Catholic Church)

The Epiphany
(Episcopal Church; see below, January 7)

Daughters and Sons of God

Readings: 1 John 5:5-13; Mark 1:7-11 or Luke 3:23-38 or 3:23, 31-34, 36, 38

Scripture:
[Jesus] was the son, as was thought, of Joseph, the son of Heli,
. . . the son of Enos, the son of Seth,
the son of Adam, the son of God (Luke 3:23b, 38).

Reflection: Luke's genealogy of Jesus names only the fathers and sons going back to Adam, son of God, the divine Father. In Luke's first two chapters there is much about Mary, the mother of Jesus, Elizabeth, his aunt, and the widowed prophetess Anna. Now the women disappear. All had names and all were essential in the human ancestry of Jesus. But their identity is hidden in the silence of a patriarchal culture.

Just as the role of the women in Jesus' ancestry lies hidden, so the feminine dimension of the Divine often remains submerged in our unconscious. Even in ancient Israel there were feminine metaphors for God. Moses in his last instructions to his people speaks of "the God who gave you birth" (Deut 32:18). And through the prophet Isaiah God proclaims,

As a mother comforts her son,
  so will I comfort you (Isa 66:13).

Jesus speaks of himself as mother when he says,

Jerusalem, Jerusalem, . . .
  how many times I yearned to gather your children
    together
  as a hen gathers her brood under her wings . . .
    (Luke 13:34).

Jesus as mother gives us birth by pouring out his Spirit in us through his death on the cross.

Mothers and daughters, fathers and sons, women and men—all image God present with us in Christ. Yet no image or metaphor can ever fully express who God is. Our minds can never fully comprehend the divine mystery—that mystery who is love (1 John 4:8). That mystery, however, chooses to dwell among and within us as One we can embrace in love.

Meditation: What are your usual images of God? What feelings arise in you when you use or hear opposite gendered images? Recall that God, the Source of all humanity, in whose image we are made, female and male, is infinite Love beyond the limits of image or gender.

Prayer: Mother who gives us birth, Father whom your Son Jesus makes our Father through sharing your Spirit, help us rejoice in our likeness to you as we welcome your infinite Love living in us. We pray this through Christ Jesus. Amen.

EPIPHANY AND
BAPTISM OF THE LORD

A Journey with the Magi

Readings: Isa 60:1-6; Eph 3:2-3a, 5-6; Matt 2:1-12

Scripture:
And behold, the star that they had seen at its rising
    preceded them,
  until it came and stopped over the place where the child
    was.
They were overjoyed at seeing the star,
  and on entering the house
  they saw the child with Mary his mother (Matt
    2:9b-11a).

Reflection: Today's liturgy dazzles us with the splendor of light and the magnificence of rich gifts. The glory of God shines on us (Isa 60:1) as we join "the magi from the east" (Matt 2:1) who lead the great procession from "the ends of the earth" to offer gifts to the Prince of Peace, the Son of Justice (Psalm 72:7-8, 10-11).

The magi "saw his star at its rising" (Matt 2:2b) and left all behind to follow its light. My recollections of T.S. Eliot's poem "Journey of the Magi" fill my imagination with images of obstacles they might have faced: crabby camels, bickering camel tenders, dirty inns, and bad weather. They must have wondered at times whether their trust in that star was crazy, misguided gullibility. But whether trudging, running and leaping, or just walking steadily on, they kept following that star until they arrived at their destination "overjoyed" (Matt 2:10a). Their trust was confirmed.

We are all someplace in this caravan on life's journey. Maybe you yourself saw that star on some dark night. It may have been shining in someone's eyes, twinkling in some kind word of stranger or friend, glowing in an act of peace or of justice, burning in the words of Scripture or liturgy, blazing in a blinding insight. Maybe you joined the caravan because of someone else's trust in the star. No matter. You are on the way.

The trip has its highpoints, but it is not always easy. Today's feast gives us courage. The magi arrived; so will we. Our choice to follow will bring us "overjoyed" to our destination with the Divine Child where the splendor and joy will never end.

Meditation: Where did you first see that star? Where do you see it now? What gifts are you bringing?

Prayer: Child of Light, you are that Star which will never set (Easter *Exsultet*). Keep our eyes fixed on you and be with us every step of the way until we come to our final destination. We pray with trust and gratitude. Amen.

Beloved

Readings: Isa 42:1-4, 6-7; or Isa 40:1-5, 9-11; or Acts 10:34-38; or Titus 2:11-14; 3:4-7; Luke 3:15-16, 21-22

Scripture:
After all the people had been baptized
   and Jesus also had been baptized and was praying,
   heaven was opened and the Holy Spirit descended
     upon him
in bodily form like a dove.
And a voice came from heaven,
   "You are my beloved Son;
   with you I am well pleased" (Luke 3:21-22).

Reflection: Most of us have a mental picture of Jesus' baptism based on the gospels, and on icons and classic paintings. Jesus is often pictured immersed in the Jordan, or coming up out of the river, with John the Baptist pouring water over his head. The Holy Spirit in the form of a dove flutters over him. On the icons is often the text of the Father's voice from heaven saying, "You are my beloved Son; with you I am well pleased" (Luke 3:22b). This scene mirrors the picture of creation in the book of Genesis. "In the beginning" God creates "the heavens and the earth" while "a mighty wind [sweeps] over the waters" (Gen 1:1). (Instead of "mighty wind" for the Hebrew *ruah elohim*, some translations use "the spirit of

God.") And God calls what is created "good." Jesus' baptism also prefigures in a powerful way his descent into the waters of death and his rising up out of them filled with the Spirit as the beloved of God in whom life triumphs over death.

Our life "is hidden with Christ in God" (Col 3:3b). Today we are with Jesus in his baptism which mirrors our creation "in Christ," and prefigures our final transformation by his Spirit through our death and resurrection in him. In this celebration the mystery of our own baptismal life is stirred up. Coming up out of the river Jordan in Christ we hear God's voice saying to each of us, I love you whom I have made; you are good! You are my beloved child! My Spirit of Love lives in you. My Love for and in you is stronger than death (see Cant 8:6); it will never end" (see 1 Cor 13:8).

Meditation: In faith open your inner ear to God's voice saying to you, "You are my Beloved . . . with you I am well pleased." Quietly repeat these words as you let go doubts and self-criticism.

Prayer: Gracious God and lover of all you have made, you have created and redeemed us in Christ. Through the light and power of his Spirit in us let us know the strength of your love so that together in Christ we may rejoice in you now and forever. Amen.

References

Thomas Keating, *Open Mind, Open Heart*. New York: Amity House, 1986, p. 127.

James Boswell's *Life of Samuel Johnson* quoted from "The Samuel Johnson Sound Bite Page," http://www.samueljohnson.com/index.html.

Bono quoted from *SOJOMAIL: A weekly email-zine of spirituality, politics and culture* [www.sojo.net.], 2-03-06.

Isak Dinesen, *Babette's Feast and Other Anecdotes of Destiny.* Vintage Books Edition, March 1988, pp. 7, 42).